HOLIDAY FUN!

CHRISTMAS

by Adeline J. Zimmerman

TABLE OF CONTENTS

tadpole books

WORDS TO KNOW

carols

Christmas tree

cookies

gift

give

stocking

CHRISTMAS

It is Christmas!

I check my stocking.

There is a gift inside!

YO!
HO
HO

We sit around the Christmas tree.

gift

We give gifts.

We sing carols.

We make cookies.

It is a fun holiday!

LET'S REVIEW!

A holiday is a special day. Christmas is on December 25. How is this family celebrating?

INDEX